YOUR KNOWLEDGE HAS VALUE

Linguistic analysis of the usage of emotes in Twitch Chat

Janne Siebertz

Bibliographic information published by the German National Library:

The German National Library lists this publication in the National Bibliography; detailed bibliographic data are available on the Internet at http://dnb.dnb.de.

ISBN: 9783346784315
This book is also available as an ebook.

© GRIN Publishing GmbH
Nymphenburger Straße 86
80636 München

Print and binding: Books on Demand GmbH, Norderstedt, Germany
Printed on acid-free paper from responsible sources.

The present work has been carefully prepared. Nevertheless, authors and publishers do not incur liability for the correctness of information, notes, links and advice as well as any printing errors.

GRIN web shop: https://www.grin.com/document/1309112

RHEINISCHE FRIEDRICH-WILHELMS-UNIVERSITÄT BONN

Institut für Anglistik, Amerikanistik und Keltologie

What does that mean OMEGALUL - Linguistic Analysis of the usage of emotes in Twitch Chat

Issues in Social Media and Beyond

Sommersemester 2022

Janne Henrik Siebertz

2. Semester

Bonn, 06.12.2022

Table of Contents

1. Introduction

During the pandemic, the need for entertainment that was easy to come by and accessible from home was at an all-time high. Many platforms offering video on demand (VOD) services profited greatly from this newfound demand. But not only did the demand for platforms offering VOD services grow, but also the need for live entertainment.

For many, the solution was the live streaming platform Twitch. By offering the possibility for real-time interaction with the streamer and the other viewers Twitch quickly amassed a vast number of viewers overall categories. In only one year they had more than doubled the number of average viewers. From before the pandemic in January 2020 to the same month in the following year, the number grew from approximately 1.35 million to just under three million (Twitch Statistics & Charts, n.y.).

Even though there has been substantial interest in Twitch due to its increasing popularity among all demographics, there is still research that needs to be done. The usage of emotes, which are a vital part of Twitch culture, needs to be analysed more, as they are often used in unintuitive ways.

This paper aims to do just that and provide clarity and a sense of understanding of the usage of emotes in chats on the platform Twitch.tv.

It can be assumed that emotes are used to either build on the meaning of the message, in terms of providing what facial expressions provide in face-to-face conversations, to indicate irony or in other ways to add meaning to the message, or as a mitigating function as illocutionary force indicators.

The paper will accomplish this by first giving an oversight of previously done research related to the topic. Then it will explain how the data was collected and how it is going to be used for this paper. A summary of the results gained from processing the data will be presented before those results will be discussed. Lastly, the paper will conclude with an evaluation of the accuracy of the hypothesis.

2. Theoretical background

2.1. Computer Mediated Communication (CMC)

In its early days, the internet progressed from a network connecting different academic faculties worldwide to allow the fast exchange of data and knowledge towards popular access in the 1990s, allowing people to access the Internet from home for non-academic purposes.

This progress led to significant diversification of internet users, which only increased with the introduction of the world wide web. Due to the world wide web, there now was no focus on academia anymore, attracting people of more diverse socioeconomic backgrounds (cf. Herring & Stoerger 2013: 2).

In its early days, the world wide web offered little opportunity for human-to-human contact, as e-commerce was the dominating activity on the web, though many users saw the world wide web as "an unprecedented opportunity for self-expression to a mass audience" (Herring 2004: 28) by creating personal homepages.

With the introduction of services like ICQ in 1996, which allowed users to engage in more synchronous conversations, The possibility of a more synchronous conversation emerged, which was rather new, with most users being familiar with strictly asynchronous conversations via comments on blogs and personal homepages, and quickly gained popularity (cf. Herring 2004: 28).

Due to this increasing pace of communication in chatrooms abbreviations, or other forms of shortening words and phrases, were commonly used in messages to ensure they could be typed as quickly as possible. This made language purists fear the decay of properly used language due to the internet (cf. Herring 2004: 29). Though Herring (2004: 32–33) states that this practice of using some sort of cypher, in the form of abbreviations, in chat messages is just the modernized version of using cyphers when passing notes.

Discussions about the effects of CMC are not new, from the beginning it was discussed how this different way of communication affects the way we interact with others, how the way we communicate differs, and - most importantly for this paper – how we use the possibilities of CMC to convey messages.

2.2. Emoticons, Emotes and what illocution has to do with all this

Traditionally emotes or emoticons consist of ASCII symbols combined in a way to convey meaning by forming faces or other things. Though newer ones consist of small pictures displaying various things that could be needed in communication.

Emoticons usually are used "as indicators of affective states" (cf. Dresner & Herring 2010: 2). In text-based CMC emotes replace the non-linguistic information, due to the lack of the face-to-face component and thereby the possibility for facial expression, gestures, and other bodily indicators.

This assumed and accepted suggestion of emoticons and emotes purpose, as taking over some aspect of regular face-to-face conversations in textual conversations, often is the correct way to look at and interpret an emoticon or emote. But often this very direct way of interpretation is not the correct one, as emoticons or emotes often carry one or more implied pragmatic meanings and are thereby to be interpreted and understood in linguistic terms (cf. Dresner & Herring 2010: 2).

Dresner and Herring (2010: 2) have identified three ways in which emoticons or emotes function:

1) as emotion indicators, mapped directly onto facial expressions;
2) as indicators of non-emotional meanings, mapped conventionally onto a facial expression, and
3) as illocutionary force indicators that do not map conventionally onto facial expression.

By attributing this function to emoticons and emotes as indicators of illocutionary force, they are not seen as extra-linguistic tools expanding on the meaning of a textual utterance, but as means to understand the intent behind a linguistic utterance (cf. Dresner & Herring 2010: 7).

From now on this paper will be using emote to refer to both traditional emoticons as well as Twitch emote, which are still to be explained, as Twitch itself refers to their version as emotes and those will be the main topic of analysis. Though different in form and makeup attributes applied to traditional emoticons also apply to the kind of emotes discussed in this paper.

According to Searle (1979: viii), illocutionary acts can be sorted into five categories:

- assertive = a true statement about how things / the world are
- directive = attempt to get someone to do something (e.g. command them)
- commissive = make a commitment to an action the speaker will do in the future (e.g. promises)
- expressive = express one's feelings, attitudes, or psychological state (e.g. thanks)

3

- declarative = affect change in the world in accordance with the proposition of the declaration (e.g. baptism)

2.3. Twitch

Twitch.tv is a live streaming platform first founded in 2011 as the branch of Justin.tv for gaming-related content. Due to the ever-growing popularity of the gaming-related spin-off, the parent company's name was changed to Twitch Interactive (cf. Hope 2019: 9). Though it evolved from the gaming-related branch of Justin.tv Twitch now features content of a wide variety of content. Gaming still being a vital and the biggest part of content created on Twitch, the single most streamed category as of 2022 is Just Chatting, a category that basically describes the concept of a video podcast (Twitch Statistics & Charts, n.d.).

Even though it is possible to consume content on Twitch completely anonymous, an account is required to access and use most of the features offered by Twitch, as you are not able to create your own content or participate in other stream's chats without one (cf. Hope 2019: 9). With an account, users are also able to financially support a streamer by subscribing to them. Subscriptions are separated into three differently priced tiers, costing 3.99, 7.99, and 19.99 Euro per month, these prices apply to Germany as Twitch introduced regional pricing for subscriptions (Wehrens 2022, Local Subscription Pricing Countries, n.y.). With this subscription, users gain several small privileges, but most importantly they gain access to subscriber emotes. Each streamer has a certain number of emote slots they can use. Starting with five emote slots for small streamers, who receive enough traction and viewership for Twitch to enable them to be subscribed to, but it goes up to sixty emote slots for big streamers with an average viewership in the thousands or higher (Emote Slots, n.y.). Those emotes can be used by their subscribers in their stream chats and other people's stream chats.

With emotes being an essential part of Twitch, most streamers make use of a service called Better Twitch TV (BTTV) on their channels to be able to provide free and almost unrestricted access to emotes. With BTTV streamers are able to choose more emotes from a wide range of emotes BTTV's library of emotes, most of which were uploaded by users out of different communities. Other than the subscriber emotes those BTTV emotes can only be seen by users if they have the BTTV browser extension installed, as they appear as plain text otherwise. But if users have the browser extension installed, they can use all the emote the streamer has chosen for free (cf. Kobs, Zehe, Bernstetter, Chibane, Pfister, Tritscher & Hotho 2020: 6).

Due to different streamers often having similar or partially the same emotes, the meaning of some classic emotes are widely known to regular Twitch chat users. This also leads to users becoming acquainted with using and reading them. This familiarity is necessary as the correct spelling and capitalisation are essential to using BTTV emotes, as they are only shown as the corresponding emote if capitalised correctly (cf. Kobs et al 2020: 5).

3. Methodology

The Corpus for this paper was manually compiled from Twitch between 14 August and 16 August 2022. Four random streams were chosen from the Browse section on Twitch.tv, sorted by the number of viewers from high to low. After choosing which chats would be used for the corpus, the data was downloaded on 16 August 2022 between 2:31-3:49 pm. The chats were downloaded using the open-source tool Twitch Downloader 1.40.7 by GitHub user lay295/Lewis Pardo.

The chats, which were downloaded as plain text files, contained the relative timestamp of each message, the username of the user who sent a message and the message itself. As the users engaged in chat while using a username they chose, the paper sees their anonymity as preserved.

The data, which was still separated by stream was then inserted into AntConc to form a corpus. This corpus was used to determine the most used emotes. To determine the most used emotes, the top twenty most commonly occurring tokens were manually filtered to sort out five emotes.

With the emotes that were to be looked at chosen, each text file containing the chat of an entire stream was combed through to find messages or groups of messages using this emote. When choosing which messages to use, it was attempted to choose them without regard for context and space them out over the entire stream, to ensure as little bias as possible.

After the messages had been collected without regard for context, it was now important to determine the context of the messages to be able to properly analyse the functions of the emotes used. Using the timestamps of the chosen messages, the corresponding extract of the stream was reviewed, and the context of the message was noted. The message as well as the context will be presented to the reader as a picture and a brief summary accordingly.

Then the messages will be analysed concerning their usage of emotes according to the different functions of emotes established by Dresner and Herring (see 2.2. Emoticons, Emotes and what illocution has to do with all this). In all cases the message will be looked at through the lens of the beforementioned classes of illocutionary speech acts, established by Searle (see 2.2.

Emoticons, Emotes and what illocution has to do with all this), and categorised accordingly. For this, messages may be analysed in small groups, if decided that they use the emote in a similar way.

4. Results & Discussion

4.1. Which emotes and from where?

The streams that have been chosen for this paper are "SPEEDRUNS (UNO LATER)" by the streamer TapL (https://www.twitch.tv/videos/1561285546), "10 PUSH UPS EVERYTIME I DON'T QUALIFY/WIN FALL GUYS!" by the streamer Foolish_Gamers (https://www.twitch.tv/videos/1562844974), "WE ARE THE ULTIMATE CULT | !noise" by the streamer Sneegsnag (https://www.twitch.tv/videos/1562902642), and "FALL GUYS WITH GEORGENOTFOUND" by the streamer karlnetwork (https://www.twitch.tv/videos/1563142822).

The accumulated chat messages of all four stream chats amounted to over 148.000 messages from over 25 hours of streams, resulting in an average of almost one hundred chat messages per minute.

With a corpus of over 415.000 tokens and only limited capacity for analysis, only the twenty most common tokens were looked at in order to determine which emotes would be looked at in the paper.

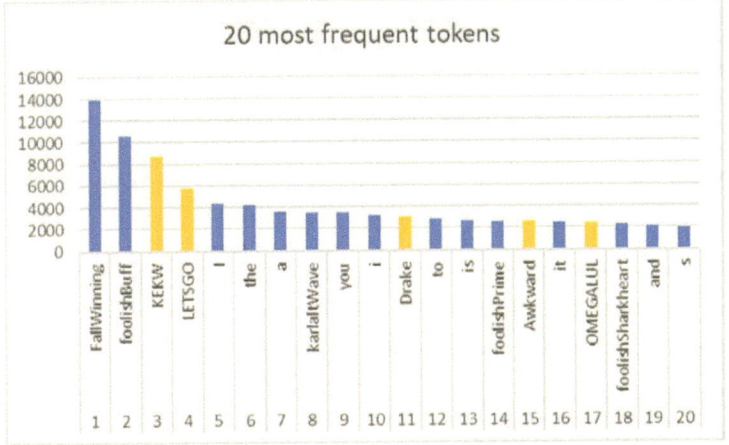

Figure 1: 20 most common tokens; sorted by absolute frequency (shown on the left axis). Yellow bars mark the emotes that have been chosen for this paper.

Of those twenty tokens, only nine were the plain text equivalent of emotes. Of these emotes only five (see yellow-coloured bars in Figure 1) were realistic to be present in all four chats, as they are popular BTTV emotes.

The emotes that were chosen to be analysed are:

Emote	Name	Meaning
	KEKW	General laughter or amusement (KEK is the Korean equivalent of LOL) (Das 2021a)
	LETSGO	Meaning and usage are connected to both name and GIF; used to cheer on and motivate the streamer and to show excitement.
	Drake	Meaning and usage are connected to the GIF, which shows Drake cheering; used to cheer for the streamer and to show excitement.
	Awkward	Meaning and usage are connected to the name of the emote; often used to react to awkward or weird messages, mostly in a way to make fun of them. Sometimes also used to mark irony.
	OMEGALUL	General laughter or amusement (Exaggerated version of the emote LUL; derived from LOL) (Das 2021b)

Figure 2: Explanation of the emotes chosen for analysis.

All of the emotes above can be found in all chats, but as for LETSGO, there were no messages found in two chats that were worth or appropriate to be analysed in the context of this paper.

In total thirty-six excerpts from the chat were chosen, containing in total 68 messages.

4.2. LETSGO

For this emote the messages stem only from the chats of the streamers Foolish_Gamers and Sneegsnag, as there were no qualitative messages found in the chats of karlnetwork and TapL.

The first two messages (see Appendix 3) are from Foolish_Gamers' chat and are related to the challenge done by him. This challenge consists of him doing ten push-ups anytime he does not manage to qualify for the next round or win the last round of the game he is playing.

    [2:05:29] canaryisles: LETSGO PUSHUPS
    [5:01:52] wikkedwytch: 200 LETSGO
    [5:01:52] PettyShark: LETSGO 200

7

The messages use the emote in accordance with the first category established by Dresner and Herring (2010: 15) as the emote expresses an exaggerated emotion that one would also express this way with facial expressions.

It is easily determined that those messages can be classified as expressives according to the categories established by Searle (1979: 15–16), as the illocution of the message is to express the users' excitement about the streamer doing push-ups and additionally cheer them on.

The next messages (see Appendix 4) are from Foolish_Gamers' stream and from Sneegsnag's stream, the decision to group them was made as they use the emote in the same way and for the same purpose.

> [0:00:19] uhmjello: LETSGO
> [0:00:20] aries_bb: LETSGO FOOSH
> [0:01:43] OneMossyGirl: LETSGO CHATTERS

The emote usage again falls into the first category (cf. Dresner & Herring 2010: 15) as they all express their excitement about the streamer starting the stream. They also address the streamer by a nickname or the other users in chat.

In terms of the class of the illocutionary speech act, they can be classified as expressives, due to them expressing the excitement and anticipation about the stream starting to the other users in chat as well as the streamer (cf. Searle 1979: 15–16).

The following messages (see Appendix 5) again stem from Foolish_Gamers' stream:

> [8:32:55] MaysSugar: LETSGO
> [8:32:55] Bay__Leaf: LETSGO
> [8:32:57] CarlyhRose: LETSGO

In these cases, the emote stands completely alone as a message, but still uses it in the same way as in the beforementioned cases. They are used to express the excitement about the team of the streamer qualifying for the next round of the game, but also to cheer them on for doing so. Hence illocutionary act falls in the class of an expressive (cf. Dresner & Herring 2010: 15, Searle 1979: 15–16).

The last messages containing LETSGO are from Sneegsnag's stream and congratulate a user named Luumeria or Luum on winning a raffle and thereby having their username show up in the game:

> [0:51:03] cabro_jabon: LETSGO LUUM

[0:51:04] morguepup: LETSGO LUUM

[0:51:04] Harold22O8: LETSGO LUUMERIA

[0:51:04] kirikea: LETSGO LUUM

As the users express their excitement and show they are happy for Luumeria, the emotes are used in the same way as in the cases previously discussed containing this emote (cf. Dresner & Herring 2010: 15, Searle 1979: 15–16).

4.3. KEKW

For the next emote messages from every chat were picked for analysis. The following messages (see Appendix 7) were picked from all four chats and will be analysed together as they use the emote in exactly the same way.

[1:41:46] Sapphisky: KEKW

[1:41:48] stephsnetwork: KEKW

[1:41:48] ButterflyBellax: KEKW

[1:41:48] arcticwolf0305: KEKW

[1:41:49] yasthebasicgamer: KEKW

[0:14:38] maria_ily: KEKW

[0:14:38] charotski: KEKW

[0:14:38] elena19_x: KEKW

[4:15:43] lumicosmos: KEKW

[4:15:44] smueer: KEKW

[4:15:44] n1ghthare: KEKW

[3:28:22] Mango_Sharkie: KEKW

[3:28:24] mrs_moonpie: KEKW

[3:28:27] meguista68: KEKW

In all those messages the emote is used to show the user's amusement about either other chat messages or something said by someone participating in the live stream. Thereby the emote usage falls into the first category of emote usage and can be classified as an expressive as it expresses amusement about a joke or statement to the other users in chat as well as the streamer (cf. Dresner & Herring 2010: 15, Searle 1979: 15–16).

The following messages are grouped as well, as they also make use of the emote in a similar way. These messages are from the streams of Foolish_Gamers, karlnetwork and Sneegsnag (see Appendix 8).

[4:32:27] allicanta: chat treating this like its a subathon KEKW

[3:00:50] miknv: Menace activites KEKW

[2:14:15] Watering_SoulLIVE: @jamiebucket, !join dont do anying KEKW

The emote usage in these messages falls into the second category as they do not primarily express the emotion pictured but are used to indicate the joking intent of this message.

Whilst being jokes it can be argued that they are to be categorised as assertives, as it can be assumed that the user writing the message believes the contents of the message to be true to their observations (cf. Dresner & Herring 2010: 15, Searle 1979: 12–13).

4.4. Awkward

The next messages are taken from the chats of Foolish_Gamers and TapL. They are again grouped together as they make use of the emote in the same way (see Appendix 9).

[1:53:06] uhmjello: thats a pear Awkward

[4:58:18] PlasmodialSlimeMold: Awkward its okay foolish we all get old eventually

[0:14:24] blaisey_bee: Awkward actually mine is on monday so he only hates you

These messages use the emote to indicate a joke and thereby use it according to the second category established prior.

Even though those messages are intended as jokes they can be classified as assertives as the statement made by the users are to some extent their observation, and thereby what they know or believe to be true (cf. Dresner & Herring 2010: 15, Searle 1979: 12–13).

The following messages are grouped together due to them using the emote according to the second category of emote usage as the emote is used as an indicator of a joke (see Appendix 10).

[3:17:55] kateslove: ohhh leaving us out... Awkward

[1:29:13] dankusbinkus: Awkward so..... how we doin tonight?

[2:55:21] junebugs_: Awkward none of you saw that

As previously stated, the usage of emotes in those messages falls into the second category of emote usage (cf. Dresner & Herring 2010: 15).

The part of sorting the messages into categories according to their illocutionary functions is more difficult. While the first message can be classified as assertive, as it states the user's observation of the streamer and their friends leaving chat out of a conversation they are having (cf. Searle 1979: 12–13), the other two messages are harder to place. It can be argued that the third message, though worded like an assertive, falls into the category of a directive as the message entails the request for the other users to forget or overlook whatever it is they want them to ignore. The second message can be interpreted as a directive, expressive, or a combination of both, as the user could be attempting to get the other users to make an expressive statement about their current well-being, or as expressing the user's interest in the well-being of the other users (cf. Searle 1979: 13–16).

Another message with an emote being used as an indicator of irony comes from the chat of Sneegsnag (see Appendix 11).

[0:29:06] morguepup: Awkward we would never lie on the internet

Due to the emote indicating irony, it belongs to the second category established by Dresner and Herring (2010: 15).

In terms of illocutionary function, this message can be classified as commissive, as the wording entails that the user commits to not doing that action ever, though that is a promise likely to be broken. One could also argue it could fall into the category of assertives, but it is hard to believe the user would actually believe this to be true, especially due to the emote indicating irony (cf. Searle 1979: 12–13, 14–15).

The last message containing the emote Awkward was taken from the chat of Foolish_Gamers (see Appendix 12).

[0:10:21] audrasia: Awkward please i don't get it someone explain

This message fits into the second and third category, as it both carries the meaning of an awkward smile or laugh, as well as downgrading the utterance from a demand (directive) to stating the user's preference to receive an explanation (assertive/expressive). This makes the classification according to Searle (1979: 12–16) even harder. In its original, not-downgraded form it can be clearly sorted as a directive to tell the user the meaning of what was said before. If considered downgraded it can be seen as stating the fact that the user wants to get an explanation, which can either be seen as making a true statement about the world (assertive) or expression of their desire to know the explanation (expressive).

4.5. Drake

The first group of messages uses the emote to cheer for something specific to show their excitement for it. They have been taken from the chats of Foolish_Gamers, karlnetwork, Sneegsnag, and TapL (see Appendix 13).

[0:03:17] boffy_m: Drake new setup

[5:06:49] honkvan1: Drake new emotes

[4:32:34] Watering_SoulLIVE: Drake that's one eyeball down

[1:40:18] OG_Arima: Drake pb

The argument can be made that these messages belong to the second category for emote usage as the emote gives the messages a cheer-like character, like a cheer that could be shouted at a sports event. Though it can also be argued they belong to the first category as the emote is merely used to reflect the excitement (cf. Dresner & Herring 2010: 15).

In terms of the classification of the illocutionary act it can be classified as both assertive and expressive, as the messages make a statement true to the observation of the users (assertive), but due to the emote also express their excitement about this observation (cf. Searle 1979: 12–13, 15–16).

The second group of messages (see Appendix 14) for this emote was grouped together as they all use the emote to cheer for the streamer for successfully completing something or winning a round of whatever game they are playing. The messages stem from karlnetwork's, Foolish_Gamers', and TapL's chats.

[4:29:46] sophiavalentina: Drake

[4:29:46] saladpotatoo: Drake

[4:29:46] EmFras: Drake

[4:29:46] honkdi4u: Drake

[0:14:39] kirikea: Drake

[0:14:40] dankusbinkus: Drake

[0:14:40] asdavak: Drake

[0:14:40] Archadoodle: Drake

[3:07:30] pitypartypoison_: Drake

[3:07:30] mimilayaa: Drake

[3:07:32] mrs_moonpie: Drake

[3:07:33] ameliaisdrowning: Drake

It can be argued that these messages fall into the first category of emote usage as what they are being used for is to show excitement over what is being cheered for (cf. Dresner & Herring 2010: 15).

Concerning the classification of the illocutionary act, the messages can be classified as expressive as they express the users' excitement about what happened. Though the argument could be made that they might also have some overlap with the class of assertives, as the users cheering

12

for it makes the assertion that something they hoped for or were in favour of happened (cf. Searle 1979: 12–13, 15–16).

The last message for the emote Drake was taken from the chat of karlnetwork and employs the emote in a way different to the previously discussed messages, as the emote is used as an indicator of a joke (see Appendix 15).

[6:06:17] BunTheWitch: george is garbage Drake

As stated previously, the usage of the emote in this message falls into the second category, as it is used as an indicator of a joke (cf. Dresner & Herring 2010: 15).

The illocutionary speech act in this message can be classified as assertive, as the person referred to in the message is either perceived to be bad at the game by the user or they are in fact bad at the game. Either way, the statement would be true to the observations made by the user (cf. Searle 1979: 12–13).

4.6. OMEGALUL

Now onto the last emote OMEGALUL. The first messages for this emote were taken from the chats of Sneegsnag and TapL, and almost only consist of that emote (see Appendix 16).

[1:48:05] SalemThePhantom: OMEGALUL
[1:48:06] sylpherstorm: OMEGALUL LILA
[1:48:06] dankusbinkus: OMEGALUL
[2:51:59] blaisey_bee: OMEGALUL
[2:52:02] Chromieees: OMEGALUL
[2:52:06] blurrypuddle_: OMEGALUL
[2:52:10] keii_roll: OMEGALUL

Though exaggerated, the emote portrays and conveys the users' amusement. Thereby it can be sorted into the first category for emote usage.

They can also easily be classified as expressives, as they express the users' enjoyment and amusement about a joke or the situation in general (cf. Dresner & Herring 2010: 15, Searle 1979: 15–16).

The next message has been taken from the chat of TapL and contains a message which is best described as confused amusement (see Appendix 17).

[3:23:17] ameliaisdrowning: you literally did win OMEGALUL

The emote usage in this message can be sorted into the second category, as it is used to mark it as a confused rhetoric question, that at the same time expresses the amusement of the user. (cf. Dresner & Herring 2010: 15)

As beforementioned, this message can be classified as an expressive, but it also falls into the category of assertive as a true statement about what happened before (cf. Searle 1979: 12–13, 15–16).

The following messages have been taken from the chats of Foolish_Gamers, karlnetwork, and Sneegsnag and contain joking rhetoric questions (see Appendix 18).

[7:22:39] lw_flower: WHAT IS GOING ON OMEGALUL

[1:23:40] matchaturtles: OMEGALUL how do u think of these

[0:35:24] Watering_SoulLIVE: OMEGALUL WHAT IS HAPPENING IN CHAT NOW

It can be argued that the messages fall into the second category of emote usage as the emote is used to indicate the rhetorical question as well as the jokingly intonation of that question. Yet it can also be argued they fall into the third category, as they downgrade the vague command to tell them the answer to an assertive stating their preference to know the answer (cf. Dresner & Herring 2010: 9, 15).

The last message to be analysed was taken from the chat of Foolish_Gamers and makes use of the emote as an indicator of irony (see Appendix 19).

[7:45:17] wynnterwolfe: I can feel my brain cells dying OMEGALUL

The usage of the emote can be sorted into the second category of emote usage established by Dresner and Herring (2010: 15), as the emote is used to indicate irony.

According to Searle (1979: 12–13, 15–16), the illocutionary act in this message can be classified as expressive, as it expresses the users feeling of being amused by the nonsensical conversation. If the assumption were to be made that the user actually believes their statement to be true, it could also be classified as an assertive.

4.7. Quantified results

Drawing from what the paper discussed previously some further results can be obtained.

When looking at the accumulated data from the previously made analyses it can be seen that most of the time the emote is used according to category one established for emote usage, if the emote permits this usage.

The data was combined distinguished by emote and sorted into the categories, emotes that could be sorted into more than one category were counted as belonging to both for this graph.

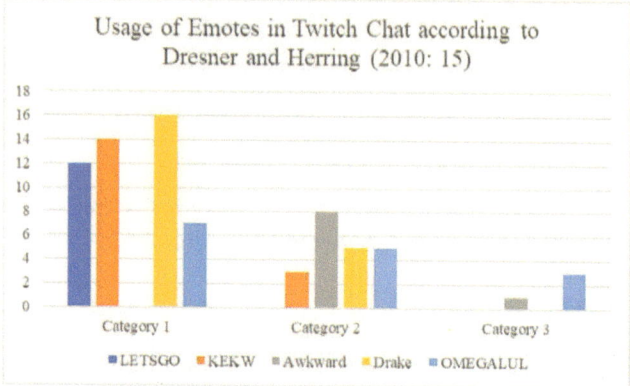

Figure 3: Graph showing the usage of emotes in Twitch chat sorted by emotes and category established by Dresner and Herring (2010: 15).

Furthermore, the function of the illocutionary act was quantified and, as with the graph before, messages belonging to more than one category were counted to both, whilst messages belonging to the third category of emote usage were seen as downgraded and accounted for accordingly.

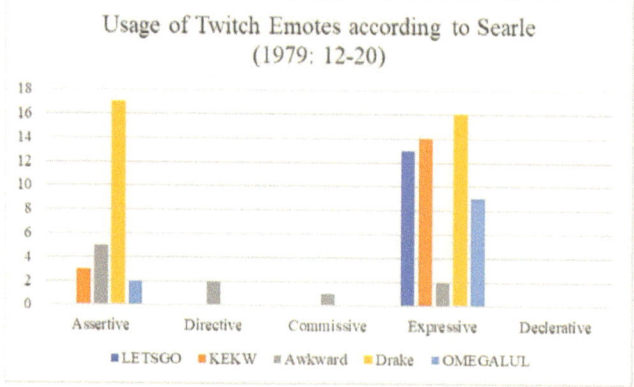

Figure 4: Graph showing the usage of Twitch emotes according to their illocutionary acts by Searle (1979: 12–20).

In accordance with the results from the previous graph showing that emotes were mostly used as indicators for the portrayed emotion, this graph shows that emotes were mostly used to express the speaker's/writer's emotion conveyed in the message. Those expressives however were often combined with assertives, as often users formulated their messages in a way that they expressed their emotion toward an observation made and stated by them.

As could have been expected there were no declaratives and barely any directives or commisives found. This is due to users and Twitch chat in general not usually having the power to inflict real change upon the world (declaratives), as well as users often existing parallel to each other during a stream, but not too often directly interacting with each other more than laughing about jokes made (commissive/directive).

5. Conclusion

Overall it can be observed that most emote usage in Twitch chat is rather simple, serving the purpose of conveying in a textual space what facial expressions, gestures or even intonation convey in face-to-face conversations.

Due to emotes being mostly used in the above-mentioned ways it was to be expected to find that the illocutionary act of most messages using emotes in those ways, could be classified as expressives or assertives.

It could also be observed that emotes showing a certain emotion or offering a clear connection to an emotion, were predominantly used to express this emotion. Whereas the only emote to be used in directives and commisives is one showing a cat with a facial expression that can be interpreted as vaguely resembling human facial expressions.

Other than expected it cannot be said that emotes tend to extend on a message's meaning, as they almost exclusively take over the function of facial expressions, gestures, and sometimes even intonation. In very few cases it could be observed that they actually serve a mitigating function. Thereby the hypotheses for this paper can partially be seen as proven.

Even with a corpus of over 415.000 tokens, it only looks at the chats of four streams. Hence a broader diversification might lead to other emotes being analysed and offering up different results. Besides this, the paper focused on only the five most common emotes likely to be present in all chats, a paper looking at more emotes might find a different distribution for the usage.

Not only would it be good for future research to diversify the data by using more chats to make up the corpus, but also to maybe choose data from a bigger time frame, to take the data from streams, where an overlap in the communities is more unlikely, or lastly have chats from streamers of other genders than male, as all streamers are, as to public knowledge, male-presenting and male-identifying.

Of course, all papers going off of the methodology this paper presented are going to face the problem that the analysis and the discussion are all subjective interpretations of a message, no matter how objective the paper attempts to be.

References

Anthony, L. (2022). AntConc (Version 4.1.1) [Computer Software]. Tokyo, Japan: Waseda University. Available from https://www.laurenceanthony.net/software

Das, A. (2021a). What Does KEKW Mean in Twitch Chat and Where Did It Originate? Retrieved from https://afkgaming.com/esports/news/6592-what-does-kekw-mean-in-twitch-chat-and-where-did-it-originate (last accessed 12.09.2022)

Das, A. (2021b). What Does OMEGALUL Mean in Twitch Chat and Where Did It Originate? Retrieved from https://afkgaming.com/esports/news/7053-what-does-omegalul-mean-in-twitch-chat-and-where-did-it-originate (last accessed 12.09.2022)

Dresner, E., & Herring, S. C. (2010). Functions of the Nonverbal in CMC: Emoticons and Illocutionary Force. *Communication Theory 20*(3), 249–268.

Emote Slots (n.y.). Retrieved from https://help.twitch.tv/s/article/emote-slots?language=en_US (last accessed 12.09.2022).

Herring, S. C. (2004) Slouching toward the ordinary: current trend in computer-mediated communication. *New Media & Society, 6*(1), 26–36. DOI: 10.1177/1461444804039906

Herring, S. C., & Stoerger, S. (2013). Gender and (A)nonymity in Computer-Mediated Communication. In J. Holmes, M. Meyerhoff, & S. Ehrlich (Eds.), *Handbook of Language and Gender* (2nd ed.) (pp. 1–22). Hoboken, NJ: Wiley-Blackwell Publishing.

Hope, H. (2019). *"Hello [Streamer] PogChamp": The Language Variety on Twitch.* Master Thesis, University of Stavanger. Retrieved from URI: http://hdl.handle.net/11250/2603065

Kobs, K., Zehe, A., Bernstetter, A., Chibane, J., Pfister, J., Tritscher, J., & Hotho, A. (2020). Emote-Controlled: Obtaining Implicit Viewer Feedback Through Emote-Based Sentiment Analysis on Comments of Popular Twitch.tv Channels. *ACM Transactions on Social Computing 3* (2), 1–34.

Local Subscription Pricing Countries (n.y.) Retrieved from https://help.twitch.tv/s/article/local-sub-price-countries?language=en_US#Top (last accessed 17.09.2022)

Microsoft Corporation (2022). Microsoft Excel (Version 16.0.15330.20196) [Computer Software]. Retrieved from https://www.microsoft.com/en-us/microsoft-365/excel

Pardo, L. (2022). TwitchDownloader (Version 1.40.7) [Computer Software]. Available from https://github.com/lay295/TwitchDownloader/releases/tag/1.40.7

Searle, J. R. (1979). *Expression and Meaning: Studies in the Theory of Speech Acts*. Cambridge: Cambridge University Press.

Twitch Statistics & Charts (n.y.). Retrieved from https://twitchtracker.com/statistics (last accessed 12.09.2022)

Wehrens, M. (2022). Twitch: Neue Abo-Kosten. Retrieved from https://www.computerbild.de/artikel/cb-Tipps-Streaming-Twitch-Abo-Kosten-fuer-deutsche-Nutzer-gesenkt-31602293.html (last accessed 17.09.2022)

Appendices

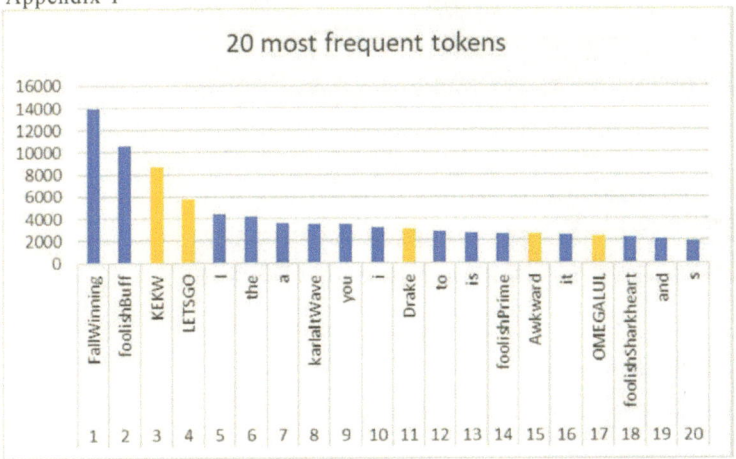

20 most frequent tokens

Emote	Name	Meaning
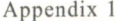	KEKW	General laughter or amusement (KEK is the Korean equivalent of LOL) (Das 2021a)
	LETSGO	Meaning and usage are connected to both name and GIF; used to cheer on and motivate the streamer and to show excitement.
	Drake	Meaning and usage are connected to the GIF, which shows Drake cheering; used to cheer for the streamer and to show excitement.
	Awkward	Meaning and usage are connected to the name of the emote; often used to react to awkward or weird messages, mostly in a way to make fun of them.
	OMEGALUL	General laughter or amusement (Exaggerated version of the emote LUL; derived from LOL) (Das 2021b)

Appendix 3

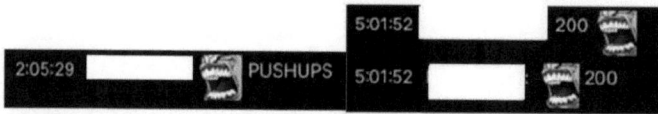

Appendix 4

Appendix 5

Appendix 6

Appendix 7

Appendix 8

Appendix 9

Appendix 10

Appendix 11

Appendix 12

Appendix 13

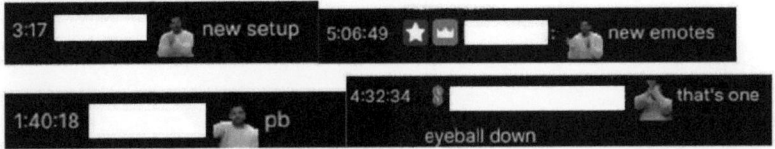

Appendix 14

Appendix 15

Appendix 16

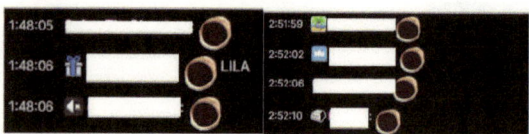

Appendix 17

Appendix 18

Appendix 19

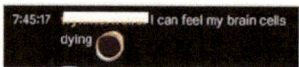

Appendix 20

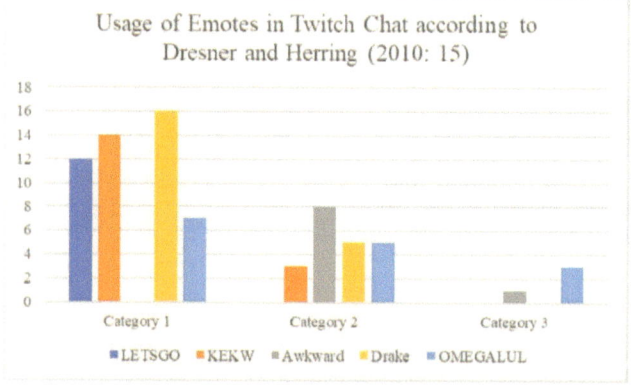

Appendix 21

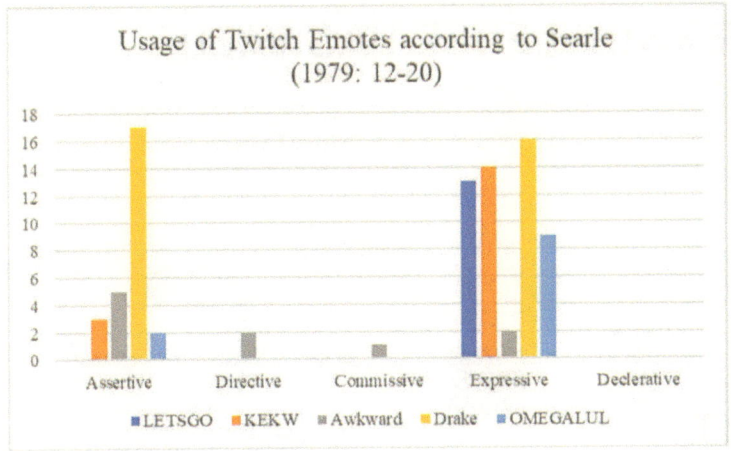

Appendix 22

Combined Corpus (see digital data carrier or Zip-file)

Appendix 23

Chat taken from the stream of Foolish_Gamers (see digital data carrier or Zip-file)

Appendix 24

Chat taken from the stream of karlnetwork (see digital data carrier or Zip-file)

Appendix 25

Chat taken from the stream of Sneegsnag (see digital data carrier or Zip-file)

Appendix 26

Chat taken from the stream of TapL (see digital data carrier or Zip-file)

Appendix 27

The file containing all chosen messages in plain text (see digital data carrier or Zip-file)

YOUR KNOWLEDGE HAS VALUE

- We will publish your bachelor's and
  master's thesis, essays and papers

- Your own eBook and book -
  sold worldwide in all relevant shops

- Earn money with each sale

Upload your text at www.GRIN.com
and publish for free